Contents

D1589559

Introduction **2**
What is a rodent?

Understanding Guinea Pigs **4**

Handling a Guinea Pig **5**

Guinea Pig Breeds **6**
English; Abyssinian, Peruvian

Buying a Guinea Pig **8**
A healthy guinea pig

Sexing Guinea Pigs **10**
Making friends

Setting Up Home **12**

Exercise **16**
Playtime; What is my guinea pig saying?

Feeding **18**
Feeding bowl; Water bottle

Breeding **20**
Diseases of pregnancy

Caring For Your Guinea Pig **22**
Nails; Grooming; Going away

Health Problems **24**
Watching for illness; Signs of ill health

Common Ailments **27**
Acci...
De...
Res...
So...

2000210404

Introduction

Guinea pigs, also called cavies, are the most gentle of all household pets. They are very placid, and almost never bite or scratch. They make ideal family pets, revelling in human companionship. They can be trusted

with small children, provided they are kept under close supervision to ensure they do not become frightened.

Guinea pigs do not climb much, and move fairly slowly, so they are less likely to make a bid for freedom than some of the smaller rodents such as hamsters and gerbils. If you have a calm and gentle nature, then the guinea pig may well be the pet for you – and this is the book to give you all the advice you need to ensure your companion has a contented, happy and healthy life.

What is a Rodent?

Guinea pigs belong to the rodent group of mammals. Like all mammals, they are warm-blooded and have a hairy skin. Females give

2

birth to live young and feed them on their milk. Over 50 per cent of all the species of mammals are rodents, named after the Latin word *rodere*, meaning 'to gnaw'. This is because all rodents have one pair of upper incisor teeth and one pair of lower incisor teeth at the front of their mouth. These grow continually and wear against each other as they gnaw at their food.

Rodents range in size from the tiny Old World harvest mouse at around 4 grammes, to the South American capybara at a massive 40 kg – about ten thousand times heavier!

3

Understanding Guinea Pigs

In nature, guinea pigs were found living in social colonies of about half a dozen animals in the mountainous grasslands of Peru, grazing on the grass and living in crevices and abandoned burrows, but they did not dig for themselves. They were semi-domesticated by the Incas and became extinct in the wild.

In captivity they are best kept in small groups. For breeding purposes, one male (boar) is usually kept with several females (sows), but as pets it is best to keep two or more females together, as adult males will invariably fight. Some people advocate keeping a rabbit and a guinea pig together, but guinea pigs are very timid and can easily be bullied by a rabbit. A female of one of the smaller breeds of rabbits would generally be the best companion for a guinea pig, but they must be introduced to each other at an early age and supervised closely.

Like many other small mammals which eat a diet that is high in indigestible plant material, guinea pigs enlist the help of bacteria in their large bowel. These produce powerful enzymes to help break down the

Guinea pigs and rabbits can become good friends!

DID YOU KNOW?

The guinea pig is native to Peru, and was kept by the Incas. But it was not as a pet – more as a handy snack, like a South American McDonald's.

4

Handling a Guinea Pig

food into a more digestible form. Unfortunately, it has then passed the small intestine where it can be absorbed into the body. Therefore, the guinea pig passes special light-coloured faeces overnight that are then re-eaten to give the animal a second chance to digest it. So if you notice your guinea pig eating its own faeces – don't panic!

Handling a Guinea Pig

To pick up a guinea pig, grasp it firmly but gently over its shoulders, and support its weight with your other hand under its rump. It is better for smaller children to put a towel on their lap and stroke the guinea pig sitting down, as this avoids the risk of dropping and possibly injuring your pet.

Guinea pigs often give a pig-like squeal if they are handled against their will – perhaps that's where they got their name! They are easily frightened, and can injure themselves simply by rushing around in a panic, reacting to an unexpected noise or sight.

The correct way to hold a guinea pig.

5

Guinea Pig Breeds

There are three main types of guinea pig: English, Abyssinian and Peruvian.

English

This is the commonest type, with a short coat that can be self-coloured such as cream, black, or white, or agouti – a speckled brown colour. Alternatively, their coat can be a mixture of two or three colours.

Short-haired breeds: Dalmatian (above) and Himalayan (bottom).

English guinea pigs are probably the best choice for a novice guinea pig owner as they are hardy, good-natured, and do not require any grooming. The choice of colour, as with all the breeds, is very much a matter of personal preference.

The Himalayan guinea pig is a short-coated variety with a light body colour and darkly coloured extremities, rather like a Siamese cat. In a similar way to the cat and the Himalayan rabbit, the development of the colour points depends upon the environmental temperature, and will fade if they are kept in over-warm conditions.

Quite a common variety of short-haired guinea pig is the Dutch, which is similar to the rabbit breed of the same name. It most commonly has a black coat colour, a white blaze down the face, and a distinct saddle marking over the back.

6

Abyssinian

Also short-haired and available in a wide range of colours, but the coat is rougher and arranged in whorls and rosettes. A good show specimen should have four rosettes extending over the saddle region in a straight line, four around the rump, and two on each shoulder. Of course, this does not matter one jot for a pet Abyssinian.

An unusual variety is the tortoiseshell Abyssinian, which has an orange and black mottled coat like a tortoiseshell cat. This type will benefit from occasional brushing with a toothbrush, although their hair should not grow to more than about $1\frac{1}{2}$ inches in length.

Abyssinian: The coat grows in whorls and rosettes.

Peruvian

This variety has a long, straight coat that needs very frequent grooming – unless it is given a short back and sides on a regular basis. It has been selectively bred over the past 100 years for a long and silky coat, and can be found in a variety of colours. Not the guinea pig for a beginner.

Agouti Rex

7

Buying a Guinea Pig

You can buy a guinea pig from any good pet store, where experienced staff will be on hand to give you advice. Alternatively you may know someone locally who breeds guinea pigs, and you might be able to find an address of a local guinea pig club from your library or pet shop – but remember to look under 'cavy', which is the term preferred by breeders.

You may also be able to acquire a guinea pig from a friend that has bred some. In all instances, look for a guinea pig that is clean and well-cared-for. In a pet shop, it is a good sign if the staff are knowledgeable and can

Body condition: Plump and well-fed. No abnormal swellings.

Coat: Dense and shiny: Skin free of scales and sores.

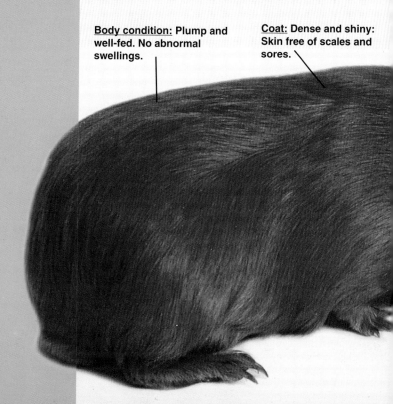

8

give advice when you are making your choice.

Resist the temptation of buying a sickly guinea pig just because you feel sorry for it – you could end up with a lot of heartache, trouble and expense trying to get it well. Select a young guinea pig, at around six weeks of age, so that it will be easy to tame with plenty of gentle handling.

Many of the guinea pigs available for purchase as pets are cross-breeds of the varieties mentioned, but although they would not be acceptable in the show ring, they are fine as pets.

A Healthy Guinea Pig

A healthy guinea pig should be inquisitive and active. Check for the following:

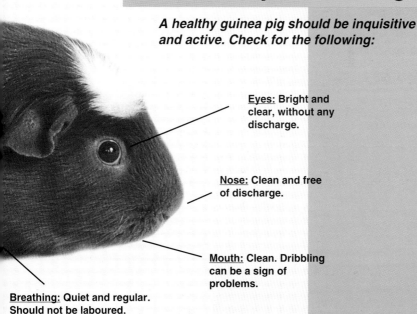

Eyes: Bright and clear, without any discharge.

Nose: Clean and free of discharge.

Mouth: Clean. Dribbling can be a sign of problems.

Breathing: Quiet and regular. Should not be laboured.

9

Sexing Guinea Pigs

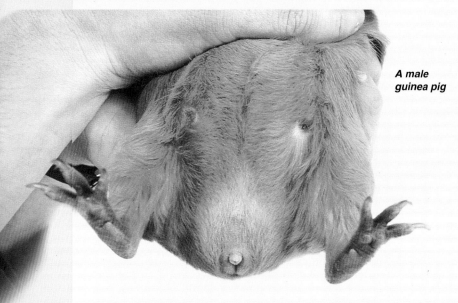

A male guinea pig

It is pretty easy to tell the sex of guinea pigs, even at an early age. Turn the guinea pig on to its back and gently press down around the genital opening. This will expose the Y-shaped slit of the female (sow), and extrude the penis of the male (boar). Males are usually larger than females, even when young. Don't be fooled by the presence of nipples, as both sexes may have them.

A female guinea pig

Guinea pigs enjoy each other's company

Guinea pigs love companionship, but if they are not introduced carefully to each other, fighting may break out.

It is best if they first meet on neutral territory. A tiny amount of mentholated vapour rub can be put on to the chin of each animal to confuse their sense of smell, until they have grown used to each other.

DID YOU KNOW?

Guinea pigs have no visible tail, but they do have seven or eight short tail vertebrae (bones) that can be felt under the skin.

Setting Up Home

Guinea pigs are less hardy than rabbits, and need to be protected from extremes of cold if they are housed outdoors, perhaps being brought into a garage or an outhouse, such as a greenhouse, with a

The ideal home for your Guinea Pig

Sleeping compartment

Secure fastening

Raised at least 9 inches off the ground

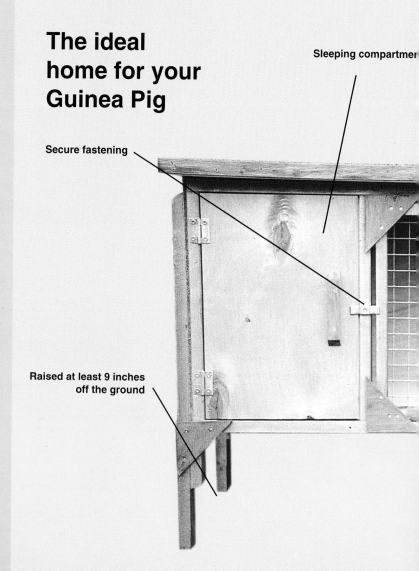

12

heater to keep the frost at bay. In both cases, take care with poisonous fumes, which can be emitted from a paraffin heater if there is not adequate insulation, or from car fumes if the garage is in use.

Size: 3ft wide, 2ft deep, 18 ins high

Wire mesh: small enough to exclude rats and mice

Setting Up Home

Wherever they are housed, guinea pigs will need a hutch, that will obviously need to be sturdier, well-waterproofed and better insulated if it is to be kept outdoors. The hutch should be:-

Size

At least 3ft wide, 2ft deep and 18 inches high (90 x 60 x 45 cms) for a pair of guinea pigs.

Construction

Two compartments should be divided by a partition with a sliding door. The larger compartment should have a wire-mesh front, and the smaller sleeping compartment should have a solid front to help keep the warmth in. Cleaning is easier if the compartments have removable metal or plastic litter trays that can be slid out from the bottom of the hutch.

Security

The wire mesh on the front of the cage needs to be fine enough to exclude rats and mice from entering. The opening front panels must be secure when closed to prevent the guinea pig from escaping, and to stop foxes from breaking their way in.

Location

The hutch should be raised at least nine inches off the ground on legs to prevent dampness permeating. If it is attached to a run, a ramp will be needed so the guinea pigs can get in and out of the hutch.

An indoor home:
Fresh water should be
available at all times.

Warmth

There is no need to provide extra heating even in winter, but it is essential that the hutch is waterproof and well-insulated. Some heavy sacking on top of the cage will provide extra insulation, which can be pulled down over the front of the cage at night.

Bedding

Plenty of clean, dry bedding is important, especially if the hutch is outdoors. A base of untreated wood shavings or peat, covered with a generous layer of hay, is ideal. The hutch will need thorough cleaning at least once a week.

Exercise

A simple run can be constructed from a softwood framework covered with wire mesh, taking great care to ensure there are no sharp ends protruding that could cause injury. Covering one end of the run with some corrugated plastic or plywood will provide a shaded area. Of course, guinea pigs need a supply of water within the area.

Playtime

Indoor guinea pigs will appreciate a play-pen, which will help to prevent them from gnawing furniture, or even worse, electric cables.

It is easy to make a shallow-sided wooden tray – about 6ft (2 metres) square is ideal for a pair of guinea pigs – and, if it is on castors, it can be moved around the house.

Interest can be added with some boxes to act as hidey-holes and some branches, together with a base of newspaper covered by peat or sawdust. Even cardboard boxes from the supermarket joined together and with interconnecting holes can act as a great maze that can be thrown away when it gets soiled.

Guinea pigs are not generally interested in exercise toys, leaving those to other rodents such as hamsters, but they do love burrowing in vegetation. Therefore, a liberal quantity of

16

loose hay spread over their exercise area will be much appreciated. They will also enjoy some large-bore PVC pipe tunnels, perhaps leading to a secret supply of food. Guinea pigs enjoy gnawing on twigs, but should be restricted to those that are known to be safe, such as poplar, or any of the fruit trees, so long as they have not been sprayed with pesticides.

An outdoor run should be covered in wire mesh and include a shaded area.

' What is my guinea pig saying? '

Here's what some of your pet's noises mean...

**NOISE: Chutter, or a whine
MEANING: 'There's danger around.'**

**NOISE: Chutt
MEANING: 'This looks interesting.'**

**NOISE: Purr
MEANING: 'Come and fuss me.'**

**NOISE: Squeal
MEANING: 'Help!'**

**NOISE: Drr
MEANING: 'I'm getting frightened.'**

Feeding

A selection of fresh fruit and vegetables will be welcomed by your pet.

While all of the other animals we commonly keep as pets are able to manufacture their own vitamin C, guinea pigs resemble humans in that they have to be supplied with a source of the vitamin in their diet. Just like sailors who used to get scurvy because they did not get any fresh fruit or vegetables, guinea pigs will suffer deficiency problems if they do not get enough vitamin C.

Guinea pigs need to be fed fresh grass or hay in order to thrive, and they also appreciate a good variety of raw fruit and vegetables, which are best cut into chunks. Wild plants from the garden, such as chickweed, dandelion and groundsel, are also valuable, but make sure you can recognise safe plants such as these before you risk poisoning your pet.

There are excellent complete foods, both pelleted and flaked, with added vitamin C, specially designed for guinea pigs, and these form a good base to the diet, supplemented by access to fresh grass when available, hay, and some extra treats for interest. If a good-quality diet, specially designed for guinea pigs, is fed, plus a variety of other fresh foods, there should be no need for a vitamin and mineral

18

Your guinea pig will be more tame if you hand-feed him (left). A selection of hay, flaked or pelleted food is essential for your guinea pig's welfare.

supplement, although vitamin C deficiency is not uncommon (see Common Ailments, Page 30).

FEEDING BOWL:
Feeding bowls should be ceramic, as this is easy to clean, durable, and is heavy enough to ensure they do not get turned over in the guinea pig's enthusiasm to get to its food.

Some hay (for eating) can be kept clean and separate from the bedding by putting it into a hopper mounted on the wall of the hutch.

WATER-BOTTLE:
Like all pets, guinea pigs must have access to a supply of clean, fresh water at all times, and the special small mammal water bottles are ideal. Guinea pigs often gnaw on the end of the sipper-tube to drink, mixing food and water in their mouth to form a slurry that they sometimes spit back up into the drinking bottle. This display of bad table manners means that the tubes can easily become blocked, so they need to be checked regularly and the water needs frequent changing.

19

Breeding

Guinea pigs can become pregnant very soon after they have given birth, and will produce an average of three litters of four youngsters per year. Only breed from your sow if you are sure that you will be able to cope with caring for her, and can find good homes for her offspring. Guinea pigs are best kept in groups of up to 12 sows, with one boar for breeding.

Female guinea pigs sexually mature at just four or five weeks of age, and if you are going to breed from a sow, it is preferable for her to be mated at around 12 weeks of age, so that she has her first litter before the bones of her pelvis become fused together. This should widen the birth canal and allow the relatively large piglets to pass through without problems. Talk about child brides!

Because the piglets are so well-developed when they are born, problems with giving birth do occur from time to time, and the sow should be closely supervised to see if she is straining for more than half an hour or so without producing any young. It is possible for a caesarean section to be carried out to remove the piglets if they have become stuck in the birth canal.

Guinea pigs should be handled with care at all times, but because their young are so well-developed, a pregnant sow becomes very large in the later stages of her pregnancy. She must, therefore, be handled particularly gently, and only when necessary, as rough or excessive handling can injure the developing young. When the sow is ready to give birth, ensure that plenty of hay is available so she can make a nest.

20

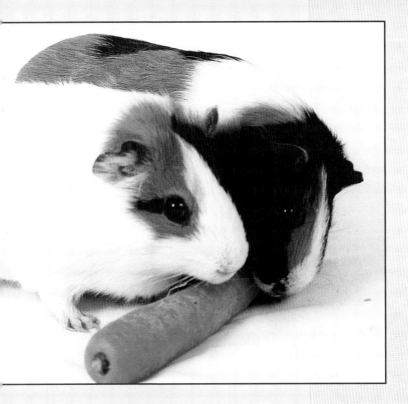

In the wild, young cavies are born in the open, so they have to be able to fend for themselves from the start. Consequently, they have a much longer gestation period than many other rodents, lasting for about nine weeks, compared to just 16 days for a hamster. When the young are born, they are like miniature adults with a furry coat and eyes fully open. They are weaned from their mother's milk within just a few days of birth.

DID YOU KNOW?

During courtship the male does a mating dance, wagging his rear end and making little hops. If the sow is really lucky, her mate will spray urine on her – just to let her know how much he fancies her!

21

If a guinea pig has a supply of dried food and water, he will be alright if left for just a couple of days.

Nails

Guinea pigs' nails often need regular clipping, especially if they spend most of their time on soft ground. It is easy to see where the pink, sensitive quick is in unpigmented nails, but it may be harder to see it when

Nails will need regular clipping

the nails are coloured. If the nails are overgrowing, they can be cut back with nail-clippers to about ¼ of an inch (½ cm) from the end of the quick. If a nail breaks accidentally or is cut too short, it may bleed profusely. This is uncomfortable for the guinea pig, but there is no need to panic as the bleeding soon stops and the discomfort subsides. Get your veterinary surgeon to demonstrate what to do if you are at all unsure.

Grooming

All guinea pigs will benefit from regular grooming, but it is essential for Abyssinians. A baby's toothbrush is ideal for the job – but make sure it's one that baby has finished with! These long-coated guinea pigs should also be bathed from time to time, but they need to be accustomed to the experience from an early age. A regular hair cut will make problems with a soiled and matted coat less likely.

Going Away

Guinea pigs should not be left alone for long periods. If they are safely locked away in a clean hutch with a supply of dry food and water they should be alright for a couple of days. If you go away for a longer period, you may be able to board them with a vet, a pet shop, or perhaps a breeder. If you have a co-operative neighbour, a check once or twice a day for feeding and cleaning should be sufficient. Make sure that whoever looks after your guinea pig knows all about its requirements, and leave the contact number of your veterinary surgeon in case a problem should arise.

A baby's tooth brush is ideal for grooming a guinea pig.

Health Problems

DID YOU KNOW?

If penicillin (the first antibiotic) had been tested for safety on guinea pigs when it was first discovered, it would probably have been abandoned as a highly dangerous drug, as it is very toxic to them.

Watching for illness

Guinea pigs are generally hardy, but when things do go wrong they can prove to be very sensitive little patients, and easily succumb to shock and dehydration. Anything other than a very minor injury or illness should receive prompt veterinary attention.

The guinea pig should be kept comfortably warm and encouraged to drink small amounts of water often until help can be obtained.

Most vets are very happy to treat small

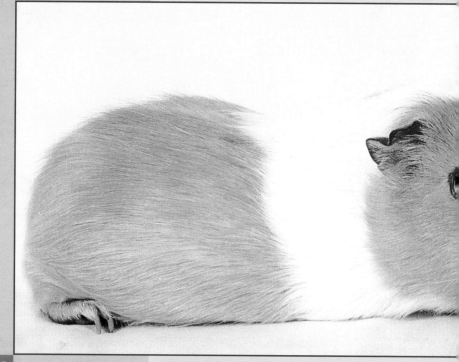

24

mammals, and you should find a surgery convenient to you that welcomes them as patients.

A small cat basket or a medium-sized sturdy cardboard box with ventilation holes will be fine for transportation, although your vet will probably thank you if you use some relatively mess-free bedding material, such as shredded paper rather than messy hay or straw. It is also more hygienic for the patient.

Guinea pigs are sensitive to many medications that are safe in other species, and there are very few products that are specially licensed for their treatment. Never give any

Guinea pigs are hardy creatures and, if looked after properly, should experience few health problems.

home medication without checking with your vet to ensure it is safe and compatible with any other treatment that may be being given.

Signs of ill health

Pet owners are very sensitive to the behaviour of their companions, and quickly become aware of any changes in behaviour that may suggest something is amiss. You might need to seek assistance with:

- Runny eyes or nose.
- Matted or soiled coat.
- Difficulty with eating, or drooling saliva.
- Laboured breathing.
- Loose stools.
- Abnormal behaviour or appetite.
- Excessive thirst.

Common Ailments

Accidental injuries

Guinea pigs tend to break if dropped, so do handle them very carefully. Fractured limbs are not uncommon. Fortunately, they generally heal well on their own with strict confinement – as a plaster-cast does not survive for long once a rodent gets his teeth into it.

If you are worried about your guinea pig after a fall, gently place him in a cardboard box, with plenty of shredded paper bedding, and arrange for him to be seen by a vet.

Constipation

If a guinea pig is straining to pass motions, it could be due to hard, dry motions causing a blockage. Mild cases may respond to dosing orally with liquid paraffin (mineral oil), but more severe cases may need to have an enema administered by a vet.

Dental Problems

These are less common in guinea pigs than in rabbits, but sometimes the teeth do grow out of alignment, causing drooling of saliva and difficulty with eating. As rodent teeth grow continually, once they overgrow they are likely to need regular attention.

Common Ailments

Diarrhoea

There are a wide range of different causes of diarrhoea in guinea pigs, ranging from poor feeding, through bacterial and viral infections, to infestation with worms or other parasites. A particularly violent cause of diarrhoea, often resulting in death, is due to a disease called aflatoxicosis, due to eating mouldy hay or peanuts.

Some of the rarer causes of diarrhoea in guinea pigs can be contagious to humans, so it is important to observe sensible hygienic precautions when handling a sick animal, particularly washing your hands thoroughly afterwards.

Treatment with antibiotics can, in itself,

cause severe diarrhoea as it upsets the critical balance of bacteria in the large bowel. However, this can be reduced by giving the drugs by injection rather than by mouth. Sometimes it may be advisable to analyse the faeces in a laboratory to try and establish the cause, particularly if there are several guinea pigs at risk of cross-infection.

In all cases, removing fresh fruit and vegetables from the diet, and restricting feeding to hay, dry food and a vitamin supplement will help to settle the digestion.

Heatstroke

Guinea pigs are susceptible to the effects of excessive heat, and this is very likely to occur if they are placed in an outdoors run without drinking water and shade from the sun. They become depressed, breathe very heavily, and sometimes even loose consciousness and start to have convulsions. Obviously, prompt veterinary attention is essential, but first-aid can be administered by cooling the guinea pig in tepid water.

Respiratory Infection

Pneumonia, an infection of the lungs, is the commonest cause of death in guinea pigs. This can cause sudden death in severe cases, or, more frequently, it results in a chronic difficulty with breathing, perhaps with a discharge from the nose and eyes, and sneezing. The condition often develops when the guinea pig's resistance is low due to some other underlying problem, and is aggravated by poor ventilation and overcrowded housing. Unfortunately, the response to treatment is often disappointing, particularly because guinea pigs are so sensitive to side-effects from the long course of antibiotics that is needed for treatment.

Scurvy

Both humans and guinea pigs develop this condition if they do not have an adequate supply of vitamin C in their diet. The signs in the guinea pig are: loss of weight and body condition, the limb joints become enlarged and painful due to bleeding into the joints, and the result can be fatal. The

disease can be treated with daily administration of vitamin drops, but, more importantly, it can be prevented by a plentiful supply of greenstuffs and fruit in the diet.

Skin Disease

This is very common in guinea pigs, generally resulting in a scurfy and intensely itchy skin. The guinea pig may scratch it so deeply that it becomes raw. There are two common causes of this – tiny parasitic mites that burrow into the skin, or ringworm, a fungus that grows on the hairs.

Mites can be treated with parasiticidal sprays or shampoos, or even by an injectable preparation that is designed to kill worms in cattle but can be used in tiny doses in guinea pigs. Ringworm has to be treated with a special shampoo, but as this parasite can be transmitted to humans, it is essential to wash your hands after handling an infected animal. With both conditions, it is important to thoroughly clean out and disinfect the bedding and the hutch to prevent re-infestation.

Sometimes guinea pigs chew the hair off each other, causing bald patches to appear. It is not known why they do this, but plenty of hay to eat may give them an alternative to chew. Pregnant sows may also develop bald patches. This is probably due to the hormonal changes of pregnancy, and the hair normally grows back after they have given birth.

Sore hocks

Damp or dirty flooring can cause a soreness of the hock, which is the equivalent of our ankle joint. This can be worsened if there is wire flooring to their hutch or run. Deeper layers of soft bedding such as peat, and very regular cleaning will help, but if the condition is not recognised early enough, very deep ulcers can develop which will need a long course of veterinary treatment.

Wounds

Small wounds can be carefully cleansed with warm water and treated with an antiseptic such as Savlon cream. Look carefully for the cause of the problem: it could be something sharp that the guinea pig is getting caught on, or another guinea pig that is bullying.